Committed to Breathing

Also by Tony Medina

Poetry
Emerge & See
No Noose Is Good Noose
Sermons from the Smell of a Carcass
   Condemned to Begging
Memories of Eating

~

Anthologies
In Defense of Mumia (with S.E. Anderson)
Bum Rush the Page: A Def Poetry Jam (with Louis Reyes Rivera)
Role Call: A Generational Anthology of Social and Political Black
   Literature & Art (with Samiya A. Bashir & Quraysh Ali Lansana)

~

For Children
DeShawn Days
Christmas Makes Me Think
Love to Langston

tony medina

Committed to Breathing

Third World Press
Chicago

Acknowledgments

I gratefully acknowledge the editors and publishers of the following publications, webzines and CD compilations where some of these poems and prose pieces have previously appeared: *African Voices, Anansi, Authentic, Big Hammer, Black Planet.com, Bum Rush the Page, Catalyst, Centro, Dark Matter, Downtown Brooklyn, DrumVoices Revue, Emerge & See, Forehead, Freedom Rag, Fyah.com, Harpur Palate, Horizon, In Defense of Mumia, In the Tradition, Lips, Long Shot, Nexus, Obsidian III, Off the Cuffs, Oneworld, Phati'tude, Poetry Jazz Kafé, Poetry Nation, Role Call, Sons of Lovers, Soulfires, Spirit & Flame, Step into a World, The Nubian Gallery, The Paterson Literary Review, The U.S. Latino Review, 360°—A Revolution of Black Poets, Urban Latino, Vibe, Vibe On-Line,* and *WarpLand.*

∾

Grateful acknowledgment to The Etheridge Knight Estate and the University of Pittsburgh Press Pitt Poetry Series for allowing us to reprint "For Langston Hughes," from *The Essential Etheridge Knight* (University of Pittsburgh Press, 1986).

∾

Special thanks to Haki R. Madhubuti, Quraysh Ali Lansana, Gwendolyn Mitchell, Patrick Oliver, Rose Perkins, Theodore A. Harris, Sheila Prevost, Maria Mazziotti Gillan, Jennifer Gillan, Amiri Baraka, Jayne Cortez, Melba Joyce Boyd, Sonia Sanchez, Wanda Coleman, Sheree Renée Thomas, Jane Alberdeston-Coralín, Nancy Mercado, Susan Deercloud, Michael Hames-Garcia, Barb Walling, David Bartine, Richard McClain, Thomas Glave, John Kilmarx, Leslie Heywood, Jaimee Wriston Colbert and Susan Strehle for their support.

I would also like to thank the Clark Foundation and the Newhouse Award at Binghamton University for fellowships that afforded me the time and space to complete this book.

Cover art: Theodore A. Harris, *Vetoed Dreams,* 1995.
Cover and book design: Sheila Prevost/ SL Prevost Design
Author photograph: Cheryl Pawlowki

∾

Third World Press, Chicago, Illinois 60619

Printed by R. R. Donnelly & Sons Company

Library of Congress Cataloging-in-Publication Data

Medina, Tony
    Committed to breathing/Tony Medina.—1st ed.
        p. cm.
    ISBN 0-88378-247-2 (alk. paper)
    1. African American—Poetry. I. Title.

PS3563.E2414C66 2003
811'.54—dc21

                                    2003050482

In memory of my father,
Tony Medina, Sr.

and my publisher,
Glenn Thompson

And to my brother,
Tony Medina, Jr.

Contents

≈

CHICKENS COMING HOME TO ROAST

≈

COLTRANE SPOKE TO ME ONE NIGHT

≈

MINGUS AMONG US

≈

YOUR PEOPLE WILL CHANGE. YOUR YOUNG WILL BE
MORE LIKE US AND OURS MORE LIKE YOU...WE'RE
AS COMMITTED TO THE TRADE AS YOUR BODY IS
TO BREATHING.

Octavia Butler

I KNOW THAT THERE ARE BAD FORCES HERE THAT BRING
SUFFERING TO OTHERS AND MISERY TO THE WORLD, BUT
I WANT TO BE THE FORCE WHICH IS TRULY FOR GOOD.

John Coltrane

IT DON'T MEAN A THING IF IT AIN'T GOT THAT SWING.

Duke Ellington

≈

New York

where the sky
is dark with pain
where rain is glass
metal and brick
where the subways
are crammed with flesh
where the skyline
is smoke trailing
up from an ashtray
of twin cigars
stamped out by rage
New York
where the air floats
like flakes of tar
where Sodom meets Gomorrah
as Times Square caves
into the pit of the World Trade
Center in a pornographic orgy
of blood and scorn
where buildings are leveled
by planes and the sun
cannot compete
or complain
with the uncompromising
flame of terror
New York
is an incinerator
of greed
a melting pot
of hysteria
and lies
in your face
with mud in your eye
down your throat
with a blanket
full of hives

New York is smothering
New York is hovering
hunched over
wheezing with asthma
Alzheimer's and dysentery
New York New York
my home sweet home
with its cracked face
and false teeth
with its steel plate head
and belly like a grave

≈ Diallo ≈

Doorway Dirge

bullets open
into flames
peel back
flesh in search
of blood and
         bone
41 points of light
leak out onto
hands clutching keys
the latch not yet
         undone
what slumps
in the vestibule
a grin full of teeth
pressing down hard
onto a tongue
surprised twisted
jaw, sparks
ricocheting off wood
and metal
the last breath of air
gasps in the silence
of a mind too shocked
to scream

Mistaken Identity

this blood wants to speak
but footprints disturb
its sleep, red brown
puddles swallow
the black rubber
of shoes too flat
to tiptoe
through a minefield
of irreversible
evidence
no hole too wide
to plant a gun
or push the sun
  through
no hole too small
to take it back
and call it quits

On Duty

We shot the
    sus
        —uh—
        gentleman
three hundred and
sixty-four times
in the back

but the vestibule
was dimly lit
and we thought
he was brandishing
a weapon

It turned out
to be a pair of keys

but in this line
of duty
things happen

It's not
murder
it's not
a crime

We're just
doing our job

THE DIALLO TRIAL IS KILLING Me

I'm in front of my students
ranting on at how the prosecution
is assisting the defense,
how they're handling the 4 cops
who killed Diallo with 19 of 41
shots during their routine
target study of young black men
who were born suspects.

One of my students—white—
is defending the 4 white officers,
saying that it wasn't a crime, it was a
tragedy, that they made a mistake—
the same as the white media and
the white press trying to portray
the officers as remorseful
and their testimony heartfelt.

I yell and scream and tell my student
to shut the fuck up! Me and the class
who were all born suspects
are ready to beat him down tear a new
hole in his white ass throw him out the
window if he says another word.

During the Trial

You could see
the point
where
the officers
created
their lie

It illuminated
in their faces
like a full moon
in the eyes
of a white mob
hungry
for a lynching

You scream and shout
at the screen
and say

See!
There it is!!!

The lie
walking
right out
      his
           face

AFTER THE VERDICT

I

You are not
breaking the law
when you fight
for your right
to be human

They let them go
They were never
going to prosecute
them

They are complicit
in our murder

Eleanor Bumpers
was a grandmother
Michael Stewart
just wanted a
bigger canvas
Anthony Baez
never had
an asthma attack
that way

Somebody's paying them
to kill us

Why?

II

That night the phone rang off the hook.

I didn't want to pick it up.

I wanted to smash the TV in,
break the radio.

The phone kept ringing.

I finally picked it up,
screamed into it.

Slammed it down on the receiver.

It rang and rang.

I finally answered it.

It was the poet, Americo Casiano,

reminding me about the rally at 59th & 5th.

After that Michelle called and cried in my ear
for what seemed like an hour.

I put on my boots, headed up to 124th on Madison
to pick her up to go to the Bronx where teenagers
took over the streets, surrounding the precinct in
Soundview where Diallo was killed.

III

You stand a greater chance
of winning the lottery
than getting justice
in this country

IV

I remembered that Etheridge Knight poem,
the one "For Langston Hughes" where he says:

Gone   *Gone*
  Another weaver of black dreams has gone
we sat in June Bug's pad with the shades drawn
and the air thick with holy smoke. And we heard
the Lady sing Langston before we knew his name.
and when Black Bodies stopped swinging June
But, TG and I went out and swung on some white cats.
now I don't think the Mythmaker meant for us to do that
but we didn't know what else to do.
  Gone   *Gone*
  Another weaver of black dreams has gone

V

[My mind turning into channel surf mode]

—This is the worst day of my life.

—The day I was born here
  was the worse day of my life.

∿

Let's go down to the rally
where the people are at
so the horses can clop down
on our heads and chew on our backs
for fun

∾

The word on the street is:
The cops think they
are the power

∾

Even a white girl said
they should be charged
with something, lose
their jobs and pensions

∾

It's not over
till the fat
lady swings

They want to
lynch our
grandmothers

∾

Let's go protest
in front of our
precinct

We'd be the only
two motherfuckers
out there getting our asses
beat by the cops

The winos and
the crackheads
and the alley cats
and sewer rats
will be saying,

*Damn, that shit
sounds good*

While they
make percussion
sounds off our
skulls

Tún Tún
Tún
Tún

blarh
I could do some
hip-hop off
        that beat!

~

The judge had an erection
when the black forewoman
read the verdict

~

Guilliani says:

"There shouldn't be a rush to
judgment when it comes
to the police:

The cops are being stereotyped;
They shouldn't be second-guessed.
They should be rewarded."

~

What do you get when you cross
Rudolph Guilliani with a patater?

A dictator!

What do you get when you cross
Rudolph Guilliani with the asshole
& the dick head & shithead &
NYPD ass licker that he is?

Adolph Hitler.

~

The officers will remain
on active duty
with pay

That's what
the police commissioner
said.

~

Even black cops are critical
of those 4 cops

They said this means
a black man
can't carry a wallet,
a beeper, a cell phone,
umbrella, keys, or
a Mars bar.

∾

Under the Prosecution's cross
examination, the defendants sat
in beach chairs with martini
tumblers in their hands.

∾

My friend, the poet and playwright, Tish Benson, tells me
that the night of the verdict her boyfriend, Kwame, a musician
and teacher, on his way home to Brooklyn, was the only person
on the train besides two white, uniformed police officers, who,
gloating over the verdict, turned toward his direction, taunting
him and saying to one another, *You think he's on something...
You smell weed? Should we go over and stop him...Maybe he's
carrying a gun...*As the train pulled into the next station, he
quickly, and intelligently, cut through their heavy laughter,
and left.

∾

Never mind baseball and apple pie
and the KKK, picture John Rocker
in a police uniform.

∾

Bill Bradley said:

"This country's so entrenched in racial profiling
that a wallet in the hand of a white man looks
like a wallet—

A wallet in the hand of a black man
looks like a gun."

∾

A white woman said,
*I'm glad justice was served
I feel safe to walk my dog*
                        at night.

∿

White people feel safe
in their neighborhoods
because they have white cops

Black people don't feel safe
in their neighborhoods
because they have white cops.

∿

We sit around waiting
for the next police
brutality killing
like it was a movie
or a book.

∿

I'm feeling good
to be alive.

I hope a cop
doesn't kill me

today.

∿

They wouldn't be convicted
if they mistake the color of
your skin for a gun.

∿

Conversation at Michelle's

—I met the cop who blew the whistle on the Street Crimes Unit.

—Yeah, I heard she lost her job.

—I saw her on Gil Noble's show.

—She lives in Harlem?

—I said, You too pretty to be a cop.

—Yeah, and she beat you with her baton...You said, *Ooh, I like the way that feels, beat me more. She said, Slap these handcuffs on me, I always wanted to play the perp.*

—She said she was doing it to put herself through law school.

—To put *more* of us away?

~

The tension is destroying
my spinal cord.

This is how we get
high blood pressure

Watching each other
get carted off by the cops

to our slaughter.

~

Since they already fear the color of our skin as if
it shines like a weapon shooting make-believe
bullets at them, we should give them something
to really be scared about when they set foot in our
communities.

~

How many bullets is enough for
4 black women & 8 white people
to convict 4 white killer cops
for taking an unarmed
black man's life?

How many bullets is enough
to make sure he's dead?

What does it take to be convicted
of excessive force: a sub-machine gun,
a bazooka, a tank, a bulldozer to level
the building—or an MX missile?

~

The movie I would make

A black man is killed in the vestibule of his apartment building,
trying to get home from work. He was shot 451 times with a sub-machine gun, a bazooka, and a tank by 4 white cops who claimed
they thought the pizza box he was carrying looked like a gun.

They said it wasn't a murder; it was a tragedy, it was a mistake.

As the black forewoman reads the Not Guilty verdict to a
euphoric white courtroom, the black bailiff, visibly shaken,
takes out his gun and blows each smiling officer's brains out,
places his weapon on the defendant's table, and says, *Now we have
justice...you can arrest me now.*

The only black woman juror with a child is surprised to learn that
her son was killed by a cop who mistook his skin color for a gun.

New York is engulfed in flames as protesters take to the street,
destroying property on the Upper East Side.

Negro Politician turns to the camera and says,
I'm the one paid to be the moderator.

Closing credits roll as a reggae-like song begins to blare:

Amadou Diallo

> *One more reason to kill*

Eleanor Bumpers

> *One more reason to kill*

Michael Stewart

> *One more reason to kill*

Phillip Pannel

> *One more reason to kill*

Anthony Baez

> *One more reason to kill...*

And the list goes on and on and on…

Cut to:

Juan Gonzalez in interview on WBAI Radio, New York.

"You have a book signing at a store called
  A Clean Well-Lighted Place."

"Yes...we're all trying to stay out
  of the dim light these days."

Diallo

as you stood
in the doorway
of your apartment bldg
eating bullets
what did you see
the flash from the teeth
of your executioners
the flash from the barrels
of their guns
that turned your torso
into a target study
that said that you refused
to go down
you refused to comply
you refused to submit
to your assassins
who set upon you
'cause you black
who shot at you
'cause you black

Diallo
I know that was no wallet
you held up to those punks,
to those thugs claiming fear
like Custer's clumsy cowboys
claiming your life to keep us
on our toes to keep us paranoid
and afraid to walk the streets
of our own communities

You could've been
my grandmother
standing on her stoop
trying to keep from
being put out on the street,
the flab of her 65 year-old
arm blown clear off the bone

You could've been Dumas
at the train station on 135th & Lenox
sitting on a bench, waiting for the train,
minding your own business,
dreaming of poetry
they still would have set upon you
they still would have suspected you
of being black of being at the wrong place
of brandishing a make-believe weapon
that is your skin

You still would have been
blown away for being
black and breathing
Amadou
who did not love you
that one February evening
in the doorway of your Bronx
apartment building
after a long day of school
after a long day of vending
just to pay the rent
just to put food on the table

Amadou
you came here
to make a better way
for yourself, for your family
like you when I got my first
job I sent money home
to my grandmother

Amadou
what did you see
that night
on your doorstep
that 4 black women jurors
could not empathize with
was it what Emmit Till saw
before he was lynched and twisted
until his own mother could not
recognize him

Amadou
you came to America
in search of the American Dream
you got what we get
every day of our lives
for being black for being brown
for being red yellow
and poor
for being woman
and child
and hopeless

Each day we bury our dead
Each day we wave goodbye
to our children

We walk this earth
with fear and paranoia
high blood pressure
and diabetes

Each day we wake
and wonder
if we'll
ever make it through
if we'll ever make it
home

America eats its young
America shits on its poor
it fertilizes everything
with death, dung
and dysentery

There is no justice
        here
unless we own
land resources
& guns

There is no justice
        here
unless we all understand
the language of the law

There is no justice
        here
unless the people
have true power

The rich will
always
have their
cops, their
guard, their
military

They will
always
be wary
of us
who have
nothing

They will
always
have a healthy
fear of us
because we see
everything
we feel everything
we smile and wait
for our collective recall
to coagulate with
centuries of rage

For Patrick Dorismond

They're all cannibals
  aren't they

Gnawing on our flesh
  for money

Reading the cue-cards
  a murderer
   wrote

Kidnapper of bones
trying to capture
our souls

   with a net

≈

How to Become a United States Citizen

≈

Excuses, Excuses

Does the taxicab driver mean to pull off after you say you're heading uptown to Harlem?

⑨

Does the taxicab driver know that you can't really afford to get a car but a cab every now and then is in your budget?

⑨

Does the car dealer know that it took three years of savings just to put the down payment on the used model you drive out the dealership parking lot?

⑨

Do the police officers mean to pull you over at the traffic light even though you were not speeding?

⑨

Do the police officers mean to ask you for your drivers license and ask you to please step out of the car?

⑨

Do the police officers mean to make believe they're searching for something in your car, your trunk, the glove compartment?

⑨

Do the police officers mean to slam you up against the hood of the car?

⑨

Do the police officers mean to hog tie you at the side of the road, and call for back-up to take turns trying to make nightsticks disappear in your skull?

⑨

Do the police officers mean to put you in a coma, plant a gun in your mouth, and when you come to, three days later, say you resisted arrest?

⑨

Do the television and newspaper reporters mean to take the police officers' word for it and launch a media blitz campaign to paint you out to be some kind of criminal?

⑨

Does the chief of police mean to say those nasty things about you?

⑨

Does the mayor mean to back him up and take a couple of swipes at you himself?

⑨

Do the police officers mean to stand outside your hospital room door claiming to protect you?

☺

Do the police officers mean to come visit you in the ICU to pull your IV out just in case you feel the urge to testify?

☺

Does the preacher testify at your funeral?

☺

Do CEOs of Big Business or the multi-nationals of finance capital, who manufacture Glocks and have a contract with the police department, send over a representative to help piece your mother back together?

☺

Does the preacher send ushers around with baskets to catch your friends' and family's tears?

☺

Do the news reporters report your death?

☺

Do the chief of police and the mayor come to your funeral?

☺

Do the police officers drop flowers in your head before they put you in the ground?

What If

What if the day your life began was the day it ended, would you think it was real, as real as a cold december morning on the 9th day of the 12th month of your 27th year, would this be real, as real as a car going the wrong way on a one-way street in the middle of the dark in the middle of the cold, would you be in the twilight zone if you come upon a car turned the wrong way on a one-way street in the middle of that dark in the middle of that cold, and stopped to see yourself, stopped to see your self, out in that cold up against that hood, getting beat, getting beat, by some cop, would it be real if on that night you saw your self, you saw yourself, your brother appeared to take those blows, to take those blows against the hood of that car turned the wrong way on a one-way street, and you ran to his defense to take those blows, to take those blows against the hood of that car turned the wrong way on a one-way street, and you ran to his defense to take those blows, to take those blows to the chest, the blood ringing in your ears, your eyes rolling back your ribs sucking blows on a cold december morning in the darkness of a philadelphia night and four bullets from a gun you never owned wound up in the bloody cop's bleeding back, would you think you were back in time would you think you were in the deep deep south in johannesburg would it be real as real as the cops punching you in your chest punching you in your wounds in the emergency room would you think you were back in time would you think you were huey newton in a hospital bed with lumps on your head your mouth twisted shut would you think you were emmitt till layin up in a wooden box while your mama cried cause she couldn't recognize her boy cryin cause she can't recognize her boy

How to Become a United States Citizen

- Place a TV on your altar
- Wallpaper the cross on your rosary with dollars
- Sing *The Star Spangled Banner* while rinsing with Scope or Listerine
- Paint each and every individual one of your pubic hairs red white and blue (in that order)
- Bang your head against an ATM door for stars
- Shoplift a loaf of day-old bread for stripes
- Watch *The Brady Bunch* for the rest of your life, chanting: *Uh, my nose! Uh, my nose! Uh, my nose! or Marcia-Marcia-Marcia!*
- Eat at McDonald's three times a week
- Name your first born John Wayne or Elvis, even if it is a boy
- Have respect for sailors
- Memorize the names: the Niña, the Pinta and the Santa María
- Snort decaf in shopping malls
- Soak your feet in cappuccino
- Give your corns and bunions electric shock treatment
- Show up at *Whites Only* surprise parties in Tennessee thrown by the FBI
- Impersonate J Edgar Hoover impersonating Barbara Bush
- Place your right hand on the bible and repeat these immortal words of Justice Clarence Thomas: *Hey, who put pubic hairs on my Coke?*
- Lip synch the entire soundtrack to *Shaft*
- Perform all the stunt scenes of the house negroes in DW Griffith's *Birth of a Nation*
- Send a bottle of E & J or OE to every Indian reservation still standing
- Hang a picture of Hitler in your living room next to the one of Jesus, the Pope, and the most recent President
- Purchase a copy of Newt Gingrich's book *To Re-Write America,* and read it as if it were the new Gideon's bible
- Repeat the only line from that old capitalist spiritual: *Oonga boonga/Oonga boonga* until you get sick, swallow your tongue, or die of lethargy
- Sell your daughter to US troops for a VCR and Polka lessons
- Believe everything they tell you in school and everything you see on TV

Broke Regrets

You know
you haven't

made much
of your life

when you live
on a park bench

and the newspaper
you use

to keep
yourself warm

has your obituary

Broke Success
a few years later

I remember
when I used to
eat sardines
for dinner.

Then I blew up
& couldn't get
    the limo
through the
McDonald's drive-thru.

Now I eat
mayonnaise
& hand
sandwiches.

English Only or Bust

We have been banned
from speaking
     Spanish
Now when
immigration officials
     kick
  our teeth
     in
we must
respond
  with
    an
   ouch
or an *OW!*
and not
our usual
     Ay!
     Ay!
     Ay!
 or risk
being deported
or have our
heads turned
into flower pots
 sprouted
with a brilliant
 bouquet
of nightsticks
 & .45s

Butta's Backyard Barbecue

my man Ra-Dizzap was bustin a move on Drainpipe. Pipe was freaked. Couldn't do shit. Looked like a deer in headlights, watchin D wax the floor with that ass—even tho he wasn't on no linoleum or cardboard, but on grass! DJ Pimpstripe's hand was movin so fast sparks jumped up off the turntable, torchin his girlfriend's weave. She didn't hardly notice, tho, since her ass was practically standin inside the speaker. If it wasn't for her doorknocker earrings—big ass suitcases, at that—the sparkles in her hair, and the 8-track tape what got her shit on lockdown holdin it together, she woulda went totally bald, bout to look like a 8-ball in this piece. But with all those contrapments, she held her own. They only had to roll her around in the dirt a few times to put out the fire. Nonetheless, Pimpstripe played on. And Ra-Dizzap persisted to try and make his way clear through to China with a non-stop leg propeller 747 type backspin, holdin his legs up to his chin, scratchin his ass every now and then to spite Drainpipe. *Fuck that shit,* Pipe yelled, trying to lasso the attention of every wide eye and open mouth that watched Ra-D spin himself into a dirt nap. The music shook the leaves off the branches of the tree, but Pipe was determined to outdo Ra-Dizzap. So he climbed up the tree, saying, *Check this out, right, check this out.* He said it enough times to get about two or three people to peep him out. Then he did a Kristi Yamaguchi meets Greg Louganis meets Bruce Lee in heaven type shit by running to the edge of the thickest branch, jumping and somersaulting two or three times, coming down in his best Bruce Lee extended arm and leg running punch and kick. Real jujitsu type shit. Only Pipe was not moving forward beatin dumb motherfuckers' ass. He froze in midair for what seemed like two months, three days and a hour. I coulda swore I smelt shit and saw his face turn white when he commenced to unwittingly introduce his dumb ass to gravity. He came down on the turntables and mixer like a ton of bricks, sending all of Pimpstripe's records flying—even the ones in the milk crates. The albums flew out in rapid succession soundin like a Uzi or a sub-machine gun as it hit its target. Heads thought it was a drive-by. They flew in all types of directions: up trees, in the swimming pool, over the neighbors' fence, crashing through the backdoor window. Before you knew it Five-O was all over the place. Motherfuckers sent a SWAT team for our ass. But Drainpipe lived up to his name. He out did

Ra-Dizzap. He drained the entire party of its participants. All that was left was DJ Pimpstripe baffled, crying and in handcuffs. Drainpipe was six feet under, takin a dirt nap and braggin. As Drainpipe began to boast and brag, Ra-D uttered his last few words in what sounded like a Miles Davis voice. *Not so fast,* he whispered, extending the thumb and forefinger of each of his hands into the sign of the gun, which in hip-hopology is the ultimate Run DMC-inspired photo-op and Yo-I'm-a-bad-motherfucker pose. The crowd watched on in amazement. Even Five-O had to stop beatin ass to peep this shit out. They all stared at what looked like a big ass ghetto porcupine: Ra-Dizzap, frozen in his tracks, reduced to an inanimate object, a fossil, a relic, a Polaroid snap-shot, a paralyzed projects poster boy, a new millennium hip-hop muse-um piece, for that matter. No one could make sense of him—of it—of what he had become. He just stood there in the middle of the grass, in the backyard, frozen in a spinning breakdance move, his entire body riddled with the phattest albums.

THIS WEEK'S *EBONY/JET SHOWCASE'S* TOP TEN HIP HOP VIDEO SINGLES

1. Every Bitch Ain't No Hoe

2. Bitch Ass Punks in Basic Training
    (From the Motion Picture Sound Track)

3. Savor the Flava Off My Crusty Ass Drawers—No Shit, Yo!

4. What Evuh It Take II Get Yo Mack On

5. LaQuisha's Hustle

6. Ode to Iceberg Slim
    (Also Available On CD ROM)

7. Man, Fuck George Washington! Big Daddy Cotton Candy
    Need to Be on a Dollar Bill, Yo! Word Da Muh! Word Da Muh!

8. HIV is E-Z to Get If You Just All About
    Gettin Paid -N- Gettin Laid

9. Multi-Various Ways to Kill Some Cops

10. ILL Literate Reprieve
    *(From the Board of Education Mass Choir
    Featuring Spoken Word Voice-overs
    from Maya Angelou & Nikki Giovanni)*

Hollywood O Spiritual Toilet Bowl

Hollywood
O spiritual toilet bowl!
O great heaven of everlasting
illusions, manufacturer of
obscene coons and vulgar
spicks, spooky ghastly
pornographic propaganda twits,
profiteering pirates and
loons, organized gangsters
selling mind smack to
the doomed

Save us O powerful
god of distorted symbols
and vile manipulative
imagery, picking scabs
off our brains, contusions
making us drowsy w/ ultra
violet beers making us act
silly and queer
driving us insane insane

O save us great technological
god lead us not into
temptation but into
your make-believe ever-
too-real kingdom
of eternal annihilation
how much does it cost
how much does it cost
count me in

Poem for Lt. Uhuru's Brother

It's hard enough
for a Black man
to hail a cab
in America
let alone
hail a bop comet
out of this
motherfucker!

Last Words at Waco

David Koresh:

    "... you're not going
        to kill us
                are you?"

FBI Agent:

    "No. We're
           not."

From the Circular Files of the Hair Club for Men

You wake from your Sunday paper
to find hair plugs in your coffee,
your shirt clamped onto your back
with sweat, beads rolling black ink
along the dyed edges of your side-
burns. Suddenly you don't feel
up to hosting the evening news.
Suddenly your mid-life crisis
makes a surprise appearance,
though you warned it against
such unexpected visits.
Why don't you call first, for Christ's sake,
you bellow, to no one in particular,
except your nosy neighbor who
emptied the glass that houses her teeth
each night, to press its mouth
to the wall adjacent to yours, her
hearing aid clinking and cascading
everywhichway, knocking her head
around, unraveling her tight,
meticulous schoolmarm bun.
I hope you get an eye full, you
damn old ding bat, you yell
through the wall, then race
to the bathroom to let out loud,
obnoxious bodily noises. *Put your ear*
up to that, old lady, you yell defiantly,
emerging from the bathroom
a few pounds lighter. *I hope you*
break your neck on the glass.
And put those teeth back in your mouth!
The last time you nearly scared the mailman
half to death, coming to the door with carpet lint
on your dentures.
Fuck off, the old lady roars, and
you can't help but laugh, as you steady
the colander under the tilted lip
of your favorite mug, trying
to retrieve the hair you paid for,

staring at your empty hand,
a coffee strainer of black ink
diluted with coffee grounds
and half-and-half.

Landscape with Usual Suspect
on my way to Detroit

Looking down
From the plane

Chicago streets
Carved into cornrows

Or Bantu knots:
A giant Christmas tree

Spread eagle
Like a dark suspect,

Profiled and usual,
With a cop's foot

On its back
Wrapping itself

Around the city

We cut our way
Through shrouds

Of icy air
Flying into daylight

Staring down
At the snowy gauze

Of Indiana

america Dis How You Treaty Me?
On Thanksgiving

they want me on wounded knee
in front of a burning bush
praying to an invisible Jesus
who's ashes to ashes dust to dust
they want me nailed to a remote control cross
made of TV antennas and concertina wire
with Mickey Mouse dunce hat ears on my head
and yellow arches sticking out my ass
chanting Ethel Merman show toons
dressed in drag
in the back alley trash of shopping mall hysterias
with bags filled with empty five-cent deposit
beer bottles

they want to change my mind
as readily as they spend a dime
or flick the channel on the screen
they want me to subsist on a diet
of ultra bright tooth paste and afro sheen
with waxed fruit for hair
and everything to despair
on wounded knees,
a crazy horse
accepting anything—
Prozac, dioxatrine,
Phenol barbital dreams

they want me to buy
everything eye see
believe what the church choir sings
bathe in holy water papal piss
to burn and hiss, twisting head
pea soup vomit exorcist
they want me to subsist
on glass & spit
on dog shit & piss
on rat bites and cat hiss

they want me to pawn my ribcage
one slab at a time
sing *The Star Spangled Banner*
with a backbeat rhyme
on the corner of the earth
watching planes and time
go by giving thanks
for the crime, the mugging
and the slime
they want me to curse
and whine on welfare cheese lines
of soup kitchen daze
in a hunger haze
bleeding bowel dragging prostate
maze through filthy hostile streets
with violent breath switch blade stares
eyes made of concrete
a heart that does not bleed

they want me to feed greed
to sell myself short to short
change my intellect and sanity
to worship their vanity
to swallow banality
to pimp smack morality
and desecrate my mind
on wounded knees
a crazy horse
giving thanks for the feed bag
empty as always
like promises

≈

THIS IS THE WAY WE GO TO WAR

≈

My Skin Is a Target Study

for arrogant ignorant rookie cops
a bull's eye usual suspect
broad daylight shot in the dark

My skin goes off in airports
wrestled to the ground
by guards at security checkpoint sites

My skin glows in the dark
blinks at traffic stops
hurls itself off tall buildings

it hangs on clotheslines
hooks itself to the back of pick-up trucks
scrapes along shitty concrete streets

like lightening bugs

it hides and ducks at shopping malls
it shrinks and shrivels in welfare hotels
My skin is used to buff rich people's floors
shine the knobs of closed doors

it's used to play a backbeat rhyme
with nightsticks & .45s on time on time

My skin is used to cover baseball fields
deflect bullets and gets reeled out
of border patrolled waters

it's full of sugar and salt
full of sadness and rage

it multiplies behind bars
gives birth to pockmarked
whip lash scars

with its sprinkler system
trackmarks and punctures
with its bones bleeding through

My skin is numbered
My skin is tagged

My skin is caged and on display
at the Museum of Natural History

Taxes

It was a savage inquest in which nothing was resolved other than I still had to pay my taxes. I tried to hold out until the final lottery numbers were selected but somehow that got delayed by sports, the weather and three or four commercials. By this time I was on welfare mortgaging off my ribcage in exchange for government surplus cheese. The eviction proceedings were swift and final. We set up shop at a nearby park, hiding what was left of our valuables in a pup tent made of Glad Ziploc plastic bags. To keep up with world events we stayed indoors mornings, reading bits and pieces of newspapers, which lined the inside of the tent, keeping the heat in. We did this till high noon when the sun began melting our shelters, magnifying down through the newspaper, boring a hole through the business section. Some of our neighbors, who slept late, turned into toast. Their charcoal broiled tears giving them a weird gentle glean of butter spread appearance. We thought they died in the fire, but were relieved to hear their yelling when, alarmed, they jumped up screaming from the pigeons frantically pecking through the smoke trails rising up off what almost became their charred remains. They ran towards the sprinklers like giant baked potatoes. This always seemed to amuse the kids lining up in the yard for school. Some kids were scolded by their teachers for talking in line. It wasn't that they were deliberately mischievous. They just articulated their disposition to breakfast treats as birds flew by with worms in their mouths. How we envied those birds whose eating habits were not enslaved by check out counters and money. Some of us would wake up early to pretend that were sleeping in order to try and wrest a few worms from their mouths. But we abandoned that dreadfully desperate attempt when we caught ourselves feeding the schoolyard kids' hysteria as if we were cartoon characters. And it wasn't such a bad idea, some of us thought, to be cartoons, finding ourselves caught up in animated tragic comedies where you could die and come back to life, where in one scene you could be blown to smithereens by a huge bomb with a long fuse, and in another get up, piece yourself back together, dust yourself off and drive off in an ACME truck, trying to run your assailant off the side of some cliff. And at least with cartoons we wouldn't have to go to the store or order out or spend our days rummaging through garbage cans for food. We would simply have to draw a couple of chicken thighs and some biscuits and mashed potatoes. But life isn't that simple.

I Live in the Ghetto

I live in the Ghetto
where the rats
are like polo ponies
and the roaches
coffee tables
that move

I live in the Ghetto
where teenagers
set homeless men
on fire
burning them
to death
for kicks

Where scag
is cheap
and crack
given out
for free
like gov't
cheese
or syphilis
or the measles
or smallpox
in blankets
or some other
disease

Where cops
use old ladies
as bulletproof
vests

I live in the Ghetto
where welfare cheese
is the new DDT

Jeopardy

He pulled himself up
by his bootstraps.

He got his first
"good paying" job
off the back of
Affirmative Action.

His gig: head of the
Equal Employment
Opportunity Commission.

He's attributed with
coining the phrase:

>Hey, I'm Long Dong Silver!

And asking the question
heard 'round the world:

>Who put pubic hairs on my Coke?

He sits on the bench
of the Supreme Court
with his lips.

His claim to fame:

He once declared:

>I'm no Uncle Tom!

Then, under further scrutiny,
rescinded and revised
his statement
to say:

>Well,
>>I'm no...
>>>uncle.

But he does have a sister
(who's on welfare!)

When questioned about her,
he puts his hand on the mic,
sucks his teeth,
and mumbles
beneath
his breath:

*I gave the bitch
some money
to get some
boots...*

*What more
do she
want?*

The U.S. Sponsored Torture Tactics Olympics Held in Central America

Interviews & Profiles

— Here we have Ernesto Candy Nuevo hobbling up the dirt road. He's missing an eye, a leg, and his left arm, along with displaying third degree burn marks over $3/4$ of his body and ant bites along the other $1/4$. He's noted in his town as a champion of the Torture Tactics Olympics, not for his physical endurance of pain, but for his motivational preparation.

— Well, what does he do to prepare?

— He asks the government for a loaf of bread to feed his kids.

⊚

— Well, what is actually interesting about this torture tactic is that Manuel, who's being hog tied and will eventually be lowered into a vat of scolding hot Crisco Oil, is actually unconscious. We're getting mixed reports from his corner as to why he's unconscious... some say he was partying heavy last night (forgetting that he was to perform today at the Torture Tactics Olympics) and drank himself into a stupor. Others say he's feigning sleep to make his performance even more spectacular... by refusing to scream hysterically...

⊚

— What has been the U.S.'s role in the Torture Tactics Olympics?

— Well, Bob, we usually supply them with the much needed equipment, which is necessary to execute much of their tortures. We also provide them with consolation prizes like free bottles of Coke and Diet Pepsi. Also, some of the guys even stay behind an extra week or two after the Olympics to volunteer to teach them simple techniques in rigging local elections.

— Sounds good...

— Well, you know, we try...sort of makes you proud to be an American.

— Well, back to you, Gip...

— And there you have it, folks...live from the heart of Central America...home of the Torture Tactics Olympics and the new Deluxe Olympic Sandwich, El Blimpero...actually made from parts of a Goodyear...

* Brought to you by the makers of American Standard Electric Chairs, the MX Missile, the Laser Gun, 9MM...

MAKING THE WORLD SAFE FOR DEMOCRACY

In Search of Saddam Hussein
let's go to the videotape

I know that's
his drawers

But that might
not be
him

Hus Se in Dat?

What chemical warfare?
That's beneath us.
We'd rather blow
ourselves up!

—Do you know who shot you?

—Yeah, you.

—Can you identify the person that shot you?

—Yeah, you.

—Is the person that shot you in this room?

—Yeah, you're right there.

—Who was the person that shot you?

—You!

March 12, 1993
Bombay, India

Bombs in Bombay
rocking sky scrapers
setting the stock exchange
on fire, wrecking airline
executive offices
in Bombay, buses
blown apart in Bombay
there'll be no checking out
of hotels, tourism has
declined, the perpetrators
have been called terrorists,
but we know better,
in Bombay bombs have
gone off, the money changers
have lost money, perpetrators
have been called terrorists
because people died,
but we know better
and there are reasons
these things happen
and there are reasons
some may die so that the
money changers lose money
so that the system's foundation
is shattered in Bombay
in Bombay where bombs
must continue to shatter
the skulls of the bourgeoisie
and blood must be permitted
to splatter so that the people
are fed, workers compensated
their children housed
and clothed and educated
and poverty dead
and hunger put to rest
in Bombay in Bombay,
a filthy cesspool

created by the vicious
imperialistic vultures
of capitalism
in Bombay in Bombay
we pray for more bombs
and more days
where bullets and artillery
do the talking for the people
and lives are not negotiated
like c-notes at the stock exchange
or colored chips on a poker table

Somalia, I Know That's No Smile

on your face but skin stretched thin
along your skull of anguish

eyes frozen dizzy from stomach growls
& wheezing

like the devastated hearts
of bombed out Palestinian children

or the choke & blood & soot
of South African babies

breastfed the blood
from coalmined gold & diamonds

I know your smile is not a smile of laughter
that accompanies the arrival of life

abundant with clean air
clean water & bread

but the cheerless gesture of Filipino call girls
sold piecemeal to American Soldiers

not for bread or water or freedom
but for TVs & VCRs & videos

nor the glue-sniffed haze of Brazilian youth
outside the sewers & shacks they're forced to live in

while tourists parade their nuts in bars
in discos on avenues with hot exotic black ass

to feed slavemaster rituals of obscenity
& pornography & torture

Somalia, I know it can't be you that's smiling
at those trained by Nazis to murder & mongrelize

Vietnamese women & children
trained by fascists to wipeout Lumumba

to snuff out Nkrumah's flame
to leave Neruda & Allende bleeding

on imperialism's floor choking on the lopped off hands
of Che, who cut down Bishop stomped out Grenada

maimed Nicaragua kicked El Salvador
in her pregnant belly

ready to give birth to science to socialism to life
ready to meet the needs of her people

swift drunken booted rapists
who treat Puerto Rico like a dirty whore

a faithful bitch
on a short accommodating leash

who carved up Latin America
like Africa into a stinking corpse

of body parts, into a trapped
& battered woman

Somalia, the soldiers are not friendly
their mission no sincere intent

but the protection & security
of important resources & potential property

an in-roads into Arab land
where Muslims are scapegoated as terrorists

& mad extremist fundamentalists
by those that created & control the World Bank & IMF

by those that want the land & the oil
& have no use for all the dirty & greasy people

who have no use for those that whine
& die from hunger

Somalia, the Cold War has created you
you are no longer the rope in a tug-o-war

but a noose strung around the neck of a people
split & divided by class

split & divided by hunger
who use the withholding of food

as they would a weapon
to force you into submission

and these are the lessons
that life has taught us

these are the dialectics of truth & reason
that blind faith cannot deny

because the flesh needs food
in order to survive

but the hand that carries the food
held before your eyes

like the carrot in front of the ass
is the same hand that supplies the fascists

that force the Haitian
beneath the raft into the sea

outside the country that is the body
that goes with the hand that covers the eyes

of its naive & gullible people
uninformed misinformed duped

uncaring imbecilic patriotic faithful
taxpayers supporting a system

that supports destruction
that denigrates life & insults truth & logic

Somalia, these barbarians can afford
to brush crumbs from their tables

they can feed you welfare scraps wrested
from their poor & budgeted

from the mouths of their well-fed
house cats & dogs

because our bones & skulls
decorate their mantelpieces

for there is always use for us
misuse and no use for us

& the world, the world
is a precious & simple woman

temporarily arrested by rapists & thugs
who think her uterus is a toxic dump

to explode their dead nasty alcoholic sperm
who think her head is a grape to smash

her back an anvil to bang out their anger
to cross & double cross

to violate & mutilate &
hate & hate & denigrate

for no reason
for no reason

but to feed a sick perversion
with violence

no reason but to bully
& torture into submission

no reason but to pimp
& prostitute & profit for money

to them life simply has no value
& they do not want you to see alternatives

to them Cuba must suffer
to them communism is dead

to them this filth is better
to them fascism in Bosnia is better

to them a free market economy
& free enterprise & private ownership is better

to them individualism is better
to them sharing is sick

collective ownership is demented
clothing feeding educating

& caring for all of the people
is undemocratic

eliminating oppression
& ending imperialism is subversive

to them to have peace is absurd
because in their perverted logic war creates

jobs & war creates money
& war boosts the economy

to them peace is not practical
& life don't pay the bills

From a Child in Goma, Zaire

I will say goodbye
to the planes
by waving my hand
in the air

I will say goodbye
to my hand
by watching it
fall off
my wrist

I'd like to live in a world

I'd like to live in a world
where the sun doesn't have
to have a reservation

where water is not
out on parole
and food is not exiled

or exhumed from the dry
mouths of babies
whose bellies peel

like hard mud in the open
air rented away
to tourists

North & Edwards

how sad I am today
at the way things change
how they seem to stay
the same, a crackhead

with chipped pink nails
and yellow fingers
smokes a cigarette
on my front steps

an old man frets
and fidgets, waiting
for the package store
to open, a skinny

boy drives by
on a lopsided bike
flinging the Sunday paper
at porches that

sag and belch
that grimace
and grin

two girls run
to the corner store
afraid of what lurks
in the wind

students shiver
and wait
for the blue bus
that never comes

on C-SPAN the President
sells us another lemon
soldiers are sent back
to the Persian Gulf

it's the end of the month
and I still haven't paid my rent
in another six months
the taxes are due

how sad I am today
staring out my window
at the way the leaves
change, their grand

green grace
giving in to
yellow

It Used to be

that watching
a horror movie
consisted of big monsters
like King Kong or Godzilla

stomping buildings and people,
flinging cars around and
taking over the world

or dark scary places
white people were stupid enough
to go in

Only back then
we knew it was
make-believe

and, frustrated,
screamed and
threw popcorn
at the screen—

Don't go in there!!!
White people are so stupid—

If that was a black person
they would've been gone
from there!

Today it's almost
the same thing

Only this time
the horror is
on the news

White people
are still stupid enough
to go into dark scary
        places

And we scream
our frustration,
unable to throw
        popcorn,

as they drag
us kicking
& screaming
into the
       screen

This Is the Way We Go to War

with popcorn on our laps
and bomb-sniffing dogs
at our feet
watching well-fed soldiers
breastfed on videogames
and violence
play out their fantasies
of blowing shit up

Every channel explodes
with hanging chads
and journalists
embedded in the
asshole hairs
of beefy white generals
hunkering to stomp
starved sleepless
sand nigger ass

for God and country
for flag and TV
for yellow arches
& Mickey Mouse ears
for oil & beer

Tomahawk cruise missiles
rearrange flesh & furniture
carpet bombs disintegrate
bricks & bones

Awestruck journalists shed tears
for the dead marine
as the women and children
of an underdeveloped nation
starved by sanctions
disarmed and scrambling
are buried beneath
the broken tooth bricks
of a devastated city

This is the way we go to war
without commercial breaks
or station identification
afraid to get up
to go to the bathroom

to wash our asses
or brush our teeth
to grab a sandwich
or pick up the phone
for fear we might
miss out on
the salaciousness
of mass destruction
as women and children
are uncounted
except as collateral damage
bringing the Dow Jones
Industrial Average to
all-time highs

I wish I Could Draw a Map

I wish I could draw a map
of the headlines rattling inside
my brain like sound bites

U.S. Invades Iraq
War Pushes Tensions to Breaking Point
War Spawns Waves of Refugees

I wish I could draw a map
of the images terrorizing my tube

Tanks cutting across sand
orange yellow flames flaring

Bullets puncture the pockmarked
rubble of palaces and mosques

As bricks pour from the black
face of sky

I wish I could draw a map
from my head to my heart
how anguish stuns the tears
that want to come

I wish I could draw a map
of the children of Baghdad
how they wait for the silence
that never comes

How they crawl like ants
out of the rubble of their broken city
lost in a sea of smoke and flames
climb over the crumbled bricks and bones
and burned bodies of home

How they manage through
manmade craters and girders
split and spiraling and sprung
through the cracked face of concrete

to find a clear flat space
in the wreckage, kneel
eastward, pressing their
foreheads to the singed tar
of their tiny bit of earth

and pray

Who Needs Forgiveness

in a world where nothing is lost
where blood fills oil wells
and saturates the land
where bombs drop from war sky
and small bones shatter in wind

What needs to be forgiven
where all is ashes to ashes
and dust to dust
in the bargain basement bin
of non-negotiable compliance

I want to write a political poem
about right-wing terrorists on my tube
spin doctor blowheart revisionists
distorting space and time

I want to right about a White House
staff with the will and capacity to
nuke out dissent to wipe away
Affirmative Action and Welfare and
a woman's right to choose

I want to write about a cokehead slacker
president with a silver spoon up his ass
and his finger on the trigger, a low-rate
John Wayne wannabe with the I.Q. of a six pack
and a six shooter in his pants

I want to write about bombs
bursting in air and chicken hawks
coming home to roast
on the backs of smart bombs
and tomahawk missiles

I want to write about Kate Smith
singing *God Bless America*
while choking on the bones
of Afghani children

I want to write about weapons of mass
destruction in my small intestine
from drinking the water
in America

≈ Chickens Coming Home to Roast ≈

Chickens Coming Home to Roast

Conflict is also a dialogue.
—Mahmoud Darwish

Our story begins with our poet being shot
on stage. Falling face down onto the podium,
his blood splatters several people
(including photographers) in the front
row.

In an automated landscape
of trucks & cars
nothing is moving
not even the hands
of the clock
its constant ticking
is inanimate
Barthelme's Dead Father
lies in the expressway
blocking traffic
the head of Jack Kennedy
stops traffic
in Oklahoma City
America's Heartland
triple by-passed
by pilgrims & puritans
& pedophiles & paranoid
patriotic Sieg Heil psychopaths
of the right wing
90 miles from Central Michigan
white power Bob Miles
former members
of the military
stockpiling powder kegs
of hate
in a country
where death makes
cameo appearances on the
6 o'clock news
where sports gets more

coverage than a rap artist
dying of AIDS
or half a million
Rwandans slaughtered to death
in mud swamps

Our story begins
with blood on the face

Our story begins
with old folks
sealing their dentures
w/ gun powder,
hurling them out
bus windows

Our story begins with questions for publishers

Free to Hate

Blood in the Face

Why would they publish
somebody who makes
even white people yawn!

in a country where people
spend their leisure time
blinking at the ceiling
while the TV tube blinks
out brain lubes

Our story begins
with Barthelme's Dead Father
blocking traffic,
the carved
out face of
the Alfred Murrah Bldg,
Jack Kennedy's skull,
his brain spilled
out onto the floor
through the drainage,
the shrapnel
impaling flesh,
twisted blown
loose & splattered
across the rubble

of broken tooth
bricks
Molotov cocktails
from the Michigan Militia

Our story begins
with hundreds of fish
belly up in the water
at the chemical plant
of NAP technologies
in Lodi, NJ

My lower back is killing me. My stomach rumbles & burns.
It is a burning silo of tears leaking out pepper spray.
I would love to crack the window to let in fresh
air but nails are trying to break through the bone
& flesh of my lower back where the waist seems
to want to crack.

open a window
in Lodi, NJ
where workers
plod through
contaminated fish
in search of their
livers

lost & tossed
among the cadavers
of half a million
Rwandans sliced
& diced & sautéed
& simmering
in mud swamps

Our story begins
with fat Puerto Rican poets
in the Lower East Side
flinging their bras & jockstraps
in the doorway of the Alfred Murrah Bldg
Triple D hand grenades
in each cup

When asked if he thought
the two suspects apprehended for the
bombing of a federal building in Oklahoma City,
Oklahoma were members of a right-wing extremist
paramilitary white supremacist organization,
the President said: No, I don't think
any of my cousins were involved.

It can be sinister
the bones of the Kickapoo
conked up through hard mud
and red clay split
by the hawk bills
of cranes drowning out
the wailing ghosts
of sacred burial grounds
handcuffed by blood suckers
w/ golf clubs
& Seersucker suits
& cleats to boot
the asshole hairs
of forced alcoholics
migrained & migrated
to plantations or projects
& welfare hotels
while farmers plow the land
& make bombs
for their very own
on weekends
in the woods
studying targets
well past noon
reading *Turner's Diary*
on how to bomb a gov't office
or printing leaflets & pamphlets
blaming Welfare mothers
and Affirmative Action
for the shape of the economy

the shape of things to come
chickens coming home to roast
their baby's charcoal broiled

in the blood of Native Americans
bumrushed & shanked
by those who shackled Africans
hanging them from poplar trees
like flags
at half mast
their eye slits sewn
& saluted by Betsy Ross
or Betty Crocker
or Quaker Oats
raping Aunt Jemima
hog tied
in the backroom
w/ broom handle
while Uncle Ben
sweeps the blood
off white cotton
& pubic hair
& sperm cells
that did not rip
through the nightmare
placenta white cotton dreams
of free & forced labor

This is the work of evil cowards,
the President says

as the death toll rises
its temperature a cool 98.6°

Workers work like 'round-the-clock
J. Edgar Hoover FBI CIA surveillance
not in the backyard barbecues of Black Panthers
or political prisoners hung in their cells
with their hands tied behind their backs
but in the aftermath rubble of cement steel
& brick held together by the blood and flesh
of babies who would've grown accustomed
to things as they are, who would've gone on
to school or work and taxes and TV and shopping mall
attitudes and mortgage payments for the house
with two cars and white picket fence never having

to get up to change the dial

Workers work 'round-the-clock
plodding through the chaos
of twisted brick and stone
vomiting the steel phlegm aftermath
of a country suddenly bound and gagged
and aghast at the spoiled brat temperaments
of psychopathic slackers unwilling
to have their hunting permits revoked
MOVE-ing 10 yrs back into 1985
back into the '70s of Vietnam Nixon & Rockefeller years
of Attica deathtraps
plodding through the rubble
of dead and gasping prisoners
to find their baby's torn & twisted limb
a finger here, part of what's left
of a face, there

Blood stains the stone
at ground zero
hair follicles
cling to ash
you would think
the little girl's shoe
belonged in a church in Birmingham
a blast from the past

But this is not
Oklahoma City, Oklahoma

This is not America's Heartland
with triple by-pass surgery
from karmic retribution
from the indifference of greed
& gluttonous Pac Man centuries
of devouring land
and blood
and bone

This is not April 19, 1995
This is not just after 9:00 A.M.
in the collapsed face of the

Alfred Murrah Federal Building
(the 98th federal building
padded with a daycare center)

This is not the 12 o'clock
or the 6 o'clock news
moralizing with the pictures
of bleeding white babies
tugging at your heart strings

This is Palestine
Soweto
Kuwait Grenada
Panama Nicaragua
El Salvador
Rwanda Somalia
Haiti
all day
every day
at all times

Our story begins
as always
with a suspect
even before a suspect
could possibly
be apprehended

This is the work of evil terrorists,
the reporters say

Our story begins
as always

Mahmoud Darwish
is smuggled
out of a 7 Eleven
in Bridgeport, Connecticut
Arafat is handcuffed
at an ATM
in Des Moines, Iowa
a Black teen is maced
& pounced upon
& beaten

like Rodney King
by Five-O
in Cincinnati, Ohio
while Dorothy searches for Toto
in the home of the Cowboy Hall of Fame
crying out pathetically

>	*O Antie Em*
>	*O Antie Em*

A landscape
of mushroomed
paranoid psychedelic
sound bites
clouding visions
drowning voices

Our story begins
w/ Congress in session
on PBS (now privatized)
while Barney is pimp smacked
& bound & gagged
in Mr. Rogers' crib
to have his belly
tickled w/ a feather
later on

Our story begins
w/ Congress convening
on democratic ways
to vote in
fascism disguised
as counter intelligence

Our story begins
w/ no warrant clauses
& polite forces
that seem out of our control

Our story begins
with our poet
who was born to be mistaken
for John Doe No. 2

Our story begins
on Channel 4
w/ apologies
from Pablo Guzman
or on cue tear-jerking photo ops
on *Geraldo*

Our story begins
with a sympathetic Ted Koppel
in Central Michigan
compassionate & understanding
& pleading w/ his producers
to cut away from the pre-empted
scenes of the bombing
& slip in the video taped
beating of Rodney King
or the courtroom close-ups
of a somber & worn out OJ

Long Day's Journey

O
J is holding a can of tuna to his head. He's in the back of the white Ford Bronco, threatening to take his life. The cellular phone rings off the hook. Rodney King is driving and, if it were not for the .40 in his one free hand, he'd slam the phone down hard on the receiver to kill the ringing. It is suspected that Jimmy Hoffa's in the trunk. But we are reminded that a Ford Bronco has no trunk. So we figure the foul smell is coming from the glove compartment. Then we hear the weird pop and fizz and don't want to believe that someone as famous and admired as OJ could emit such a powerful and obnoxious odor. We tried to sneak a glance his way and were relieved to find that it was just the can of tuna split open in the vice grip of his nervous, clumsy King Kong palm. Tuna water dribbled down to his elbow as he sweated profusely, praying that the split open can would not cut his pretty face. *When this is all over, I still want to be able to get a job,* he told us. Just above our heads propellers chop away at the air. A helicopter lands on the roof of the car. *Come out with your hands up!* comes the cry from a bullhorn. Jimmy Hoffa, sautéed in John F. Kennedy's blood in the glove compartment of the white Ford Bronco, suddenly turns into James Cagney. He is animated. *Ooooh...You'll never take me alive....Ooooh!* Rodney King takes the .40 of Mad Dog and douses it onto the hood of the car, flicking his cigarette out the window to make a fire just in case they send SWAT men down onto the hood. The helicopter is immediately engulfed in flames, the SWAT team trapped in a flying open furnace. It hurls away into a ball of flames, shooting out like a meteor, landing like a godsend in Compton, its parts to be picked away like meat off a turkey bone at a homeless shelter on Thanksgiving Day. Rodney King continues to drive, tapping the bottle for leftover drops. Jimmy Hoffa roasting on a spit in the glove compartment. The heat from the hood of the car basting him. *Damn! Smells like ribs in there,* King groans, fussing with the doorknob of the glove compartment. He loses control of the white Ford Bronco, crashing across guardrails. OJ nicks his face with the blade of the split open can of tuna. *Fuck!* he yells, blood spraying all over the inside of the white Ford Bronco. Miraculously enough, we end up in front of OJ's house on his front lawn. The car engine is dead. It grows cold inside. Ice starts to form on Jimmy Hoffa's body parts. Cops spring out from everywhere: behind bushes, parachuting off the roof, vehicles skidding up onto the lawn, blocking us in. Within minutes we are in Mai Li. I awake to find myself in the glove compartment, shivering. Jimmy Hoffa

lies next to me sautéing in the blood of John F. Kennedy, smelling of day-old tuna. Outside, King is dragged out the driver's side of the car. Hundreds of cops appear, turning his head into a percussion instrument as nosy pedestrians begin a euphoric rumba off the sounds the nightsticks make against his skull. The cops continue this until they capture the rhythm of the crowd's dancing. By the time I stick my head out of the glove compartment of the white Ford Bronco to see what's happening, OJ is whimpering because no one's paying attention to him. (People no longer cared whether or not he pimp smacked a Barbie doll in a window display case at FAO Schwartz.) His large frame broken down into an endless bouquet of sobs. His tears overflow the can of tuna, flooding the car and raising the temperature while Jimmy Hoffa melts away into John F. Kennedy's blood until a pool of it spills out onto the lawn, washing away the dancing euphoric crowd as Rodney King is being lifted up onto the hood of the car with nightsticks. For a second, in midair, just before hitting the trunk, he looks like The Good Thief, or The Bad Thief (both of whom stood on either side of Christ on the cross), or Christ himself, innocently pleading, trying not to look surprised when they begin to douse him with gasoline and press a cigarette into the air.

Off in the distance, people will steal TVs and stereo equipment from OJ's house. No one will go near the refrigerator.

aFTER THE VERDICT

When the verdict
was read
& OJ was acquitted
Black people cheered
while White people jeered,

their faces glum & pale
unlike the one's found
flashing their blood-stained
teeth
in the photos
of lynchings.

Uncle Thomas Goes to Washing Ton of Blackface from His Soul

Clarence Thomas is upon us
Clarence Thomas is upon us
not among us   not among us
a faithful slave
is rubbing elbows
in the White House
latrine, a human
Pez dispenser
he's a riot
at private cocktail
parties, him head cranked
back: mouth wide open
beneath the white ass
of the *Constitution*
he upholds
with him lips,
white wolves
snappin at he hiney
watch him give a popeyed jig
bootstrap chopped butt de Hottentot hustle
he likes music
don't you know
he'd even point you out
for a dollar;
Clarence Thomas
trained to harm us
lookin black &
sleepin white
the Christian right
a captured coon
to add to our plight,
the noose is tight
& getting tighter
it's obvious
that this motherfucker's
been dead
for quite some time

somebody wake him up
for his own coon fry!
a snake in the grass
a pitchfork up our ass
an unoriginal thinker
an outhouse slave stinker
a dull smiling neon pooper scooper
for the New World Order!
an advocator of secret trials
5 minutes away from slavery:
he'll harm us
Clarence Thomas
will bomb us
(him like napalm!)
& all the other
Uncle Thomas' English muffins
waiting like talking wind-up dolls
in the wings of the white house
to tell us to be cool
while we drown
in the hot lava bullshit
of their madness
& America's true potential
is stunted
while color becomes a blind trust
bargaining chip & symbol of supremacy
for bourgeois right-wing reactionary
manipulation & profit

The Big House Revisited

Bigger Thomas
wasn't suppose
to make it
to the big house
sippin tea
with Miss Anne
& Sydney Poitier
& Botswana
but he did
& became
a modern day
Mandingo
w/ 3 legs
& small change
& big chains
clamped around
his neck
presupposing the noose
wrapped tight
around his nuts
w/ a media blitz
& crew cut fits
& tears imprisoned
in the slits
of his eyes
& funeral procession
rides with a barrel
to his head
going far
going far
in a car with no wheels
in a plane with no wings
towards a sky with no stars
but one big ass sun
melting his dreams away
on the front page
of a back alley rag
in stereo

with a light
in his face
and a mic
to record
the pace
of his heart
stuck high
in his throat
Bigger Thomas
wasn't suppose
to make it
to the big house

Not the Bigger
from the hood
who was taught
in school
that he would
amount to nothing good
that black was bad
& white was good
the Bigger paralyzed
by white supremacy
who smothered Mary Dalton
out of fear
demonized Bigger
who was looked at
as ape as rapist
the Bigger who bashed
black Bessie's face in
with a brick
not the Bigger that was
trained to be sick
but the Bigger
who was smaller
the Bigger who was
a belly crawler
a coke-bottled pubic-haired
shit grinnin shit talkin scab
leaving his sister in a Welfare hotel
while he sits twiddling his thumbs

on supreme court benches
with the rest of the outhouse wenches & henches
& stenches reeking of hypocrisy & injustice

Nor the Bigger
who once wrote of ambulances
not comin for niggers tonight
who couldn't play jazz
& became a critic
but was so short
he ended up being
a backward backbiting tic
in the flea collar
of right-wing neo-con twits
always bitter & always wrong
but still
writing notes
for votes
from the white litter rotty
volunteering to be a hanging judge
he hate black so much
he turnin white now
ain't karma a bitch!

Or the Bigger who write for the *Daily News*
the one who stole Earl Caldwell's job
the one Baraka called a *safe knee-grow*
the one that look & talk like Foghorn Leghorn,
        I SAY!   I SAY!

Not Bigger twirling in the air
swatting Haitian slave labor made balls
with bats after the media assassinated
him after the mob assassinated
him father framing a poor white boy
& Bigger
or the Bigger twirling on stage
marrying Elvis' daughter
after the press pressed him
into press conferences
to pay for pedophile
dis charges

But the Bigger
in bars
where bookstores
& libraries should be
the Bigger
behind bars
w/ James Brown
& Mike Tyson
or those babies
I read for in the Bronx
at Spofford
the over 60%
of Biggers
who leave their mother's womb
& no sooner pass the corner curb
before getting carted away to jail
on the front page
of the six o'clock news
like yesterday's deposit bottles
cashed in for privatized prisons
& construction contracts
& a reserve army of slave labor
baited by imported crack
& junk & lifestyles
on the silver screen
on the boob tube
& the streets
they call their school
creating jobs
where they don't exist
selling for the man
executing his plan
to execute the poor
who want to obliterate
the memory of poverty
& bleed workers of hard work
and an illusory sense of stability
to have them feel helpless & unsafe
in their neighborhoods or their homes
blaming youth bitterly criticizing youth
the working class

whose taxes pay
the salaries
of the police
who sweep
our broken youth
off the curb
from selling poor
people herb
where they'll have
a new job
w/ no pay & no benefits
to benefit
the State & capital
psyching out
our youth
to have them
think that
this is what
it takes
to be a man

Nah, Bigger Thomas
wasn't suppose
to make it
to the big house
w/ Rochester
& Man Tan
w/ Cleotis
& Sir Han Sir Han
workin for the man
to keep the hand
rockin the cradle

Not Bigger
runnin w/ a ball
through airports
or leaving his wife
to snort up white whores
at cocktail parties
w/ Richard Pryor & Jim Brown
back slappin Barbies
giving other men head

in their wedding gowns

The Bigger they want
gots to put his soul on ice
gots to crave lice
over wife
over life
a shrimp to eat
small fish to fry
that stinks on ice
whose life's a lie

The Bigger they want
wants nothin to do
with the hood

The Bigger they want
believes black is bad
& white is good

The Bigger they want
act silly
& gives big neon plastic smiles
in the movies
on TV
or at the MLA conference

The Bigger they want
gots to be a good
lay
on command
to be able to allow
for the man
to take his hands
off the strings
enough to dip
into his stash

Bigger can't have chump change
Bigger is chump change
Bigger is chump
Bigger don't want change
in Capitalist America

The Bigger they want
be on *Time* magazine
with a penciled-in
five-day growth
straddled atop the Empire State Building
swatting helicopters like flies
never letting go
he white woman

Bigger Thomas
wasn't suppose
to make it
to the big house
sippin tea
with Miss Anne
& Sydney Poitier
& Botswana

Nah, Bigger Thomas
wasn't suppose
to make it
to the big house
Bigger Thomas
was born
there
& he will
die there
if he don't really mature
and change into the man
he's suppose to be
without strings
attached
bein everybody's
big tom

aNITA HILL on PRESIDENT CLINTON's eXTRACURRICULAR aCTIVITIES IN THE ORAL OFFICE

Yeah, he came at me
with a Coke bottle
and a hangman's noose,
yelling: *Hee Haw!!!*
and calling me Black Bessie!

Cleaning the White House Latrine: The Last Years of Clarence Thomas

Supreme Court Justice Clarence Thomas retired today, loosening the noose around black people's necks. Upon stepping down from the bench, the graying Thomas said to Colin Powell, anchor of the new *Essence* half-hour celebrity talk show co-produced by Oprah Winfrey and Bill Cosby, "I took a wallop from black people all my life. Whites were the only one's that truly embraced me...I mean when I reached out to Anita—"

"You mean with the Coke bottle?" Powell interjected.

In another clip from the interview a somber Powell pressed, "You regret being called a Tom?"

"My mother should've named me something else. She should've seen it coming!"

What was most penetrating about Powell's interview was that he got Thomas to reveal never-before-mentioned secrets about his past, an experience he had with J. Edgar Hoover which appears in his newly released memoir *Cleaning the White House Latrine* says plenty, proving to be most compelling and revealing. "We saw each other on occasion. But I was an idealistic youth, fresh out of law school and I just couldn't wear garter belts; they made my legs itch, and I could barely get my feet into them pumps. They killed my corns. You should've seen the blisters on my toes, all swolled up and pulsating! Looked like corn-on-the-cobs!"

Toward the end of the segment, Powell and a camera crew escorted Thomas to a cemetery where he broke down in front of two unmarked graves believed to be where his mother and sister ended up after their long bout with Welfare. A broken down Thomas said through a rainforest of crocodile tears: "To my mother and sister who I left on Welfare...ignore what happened—I was on my period."

Notes on a Hanging Judge

Judge Sabo's
an accomplished liar,
Death's architect,
The Devil's physician,
Satan's pinch hitter,
shoe shiner of doom,
the maitre d' of nightmare,
torture's midwife,
hysteria's chauffeur,
a disease on the heel of famine,
the butler of bad news—
guilty of causing trouble,
a cheap nickel & dime
seamstress sewing eyelids
in morgues,
stealing the nickels
from dead peoples' eyes,
eternal member of the Fraternal
Order of Pigs, wallowing
in the mud of corruption,
sending $3^1/2$ baseball line-ups
from the Negro Leagues
to death,
score keeper of misery
who validates parking
in the hereafter
who takes dictation
from the lips of evil,
horsewhipping hope
for an extra part-time salary,
gracious host to life-threatening diseases,
who throws house parties
in his small intestine
for maggots
so they can feel
at home,
who writes obituaries
for children not yet born,

whose judicial review reads
like the screenplay of
The Faces of Death
(where you can't miss his name,
permanently graffitied and
juxtaposed as the credits roll),
a state sanctioned serial killer
authorizing bloodlettings
as if they were holy communion,
bringing the church & state together
in a sick baptismal orgy
of Herodinus despair,
euphoric with flashing fangs
and drooling tongue
who's so patriotically perverse
and sickly demented
that before every judicial decision
pertaining to a person's life
Nixon appears to him
in an apparition saying:
Give 'em hell, Harry!
A devil-may-care rude, uncouth
impolitic barroom psychopath
crippled with ill emotions
and equally ill intent,
attributed with coining
the phrase: *Heads will roll!*
and inspiring the line:
It's enough to make you sick.
His mind is a one-judge town
and his mental capacity
gives him the audacity
to sleep and pass judgment
simultaneously while
passing gas through his mouth,
nodding off in his own slobber,
a pathetic sociopath
who polishes the DA's nutsack hairs
with his tongue and forefinger
who gives out merit badges

for outstanding achievement
in police brutality
who uses his false teeth
for a gavel, marking his bench
with warrants and dates with death
as if they were notches on his belt,
a devil in a black robe and
blood-soaked wing-tip shoes,
no mystery to anyone
familiar with the history
of US jurisprudence
who refuses to recuse
or retire himself from the bench
for fear he might miss out
on a prisoner's forced expiration date
as if it were the winning number
on a lottery ticket
whose eating habits were made into
a major motion picture
starring Anthony Hopkins
entitled *Silence of the Lambs*
whose favorite song
is the theme song
to *The Exorcist*
whose sexual hang-ups
do not include
sodomizing barnyard animals,
groping little boys in confessionals,
and masturbating to the background
music of *Night of the Living Dead*
whose picture appears
beside the word *necrophiliac*
in any foreign or domestic dictionary
who decreed it illegal
to be happy
whose cheap Woolworth's
driver's license photo
is standard advertisement
for the yearbook photos
at Mass Murder State College

whose high school senior class
voted him most likely to hate
who only mourns
when someone dies
with a smile on their face
who's so cunning
he can invade the psyche,
spirit, and mental energy
of disgruntled postal employees
through hypnotism
and mental telepathy
whose vision
(like his memory)
is failing but is still
easily bothered
by people he perceives
to be in the vertical position
(unless their legs are dangling
in midair, defying perpendicularity),
volunteer salesman of coffins,
elevator operator to morgues,
low-paid museum guard of mortuaries,
the Uncle Sam recruitment officer
for maggot world supremacy,
the skull and cross bones
poster boy for poison
who was escorted to his
high school senior prom
by the Grim Reaper
whose mother was a mummy
raped through the ace bandages
and strips of gauze by Dracula,
King Kong and the Werewolf,
and whose combined sperm
made it through
to form him,
Judge Sabo,
timekeeper at the gates of hell,
umpire and referee of
sadomasochistic suicidal ritual,

judge, jury, and executioner
of living dreams
who cannot sleep
while someone else
is breathing
who's so vile
and senile
he thinks he's his own father,
a no-name, low-life
gas chamber cleaning attendant
at Auschwitz, laughing
in the blood red snow
of other people's ashes

The Grinch Re-Formed

Newt Gingrich,
a neutered grinch,
gangrened paranoid
schizophrenic poster boy
for Quaker Oats

he worships shit,
                 no shit!
& even prays
on toilet bowls

while his mama hides
behind a see-through
shower curtain
chain smoking
smoke signals

looking out
bathroom windows
at middle-aged
Middle American
white women
on their way
to shopping malls
using the skulls
of Welfare recipients
as stepping stones
or speed bumps
& parking meters.

Newt Gingrich
(Nuke Green Rich),
a neutered grinch
a robbing hood
who steals
from the poor
to give to the rich
pimp smacking Barney
from a short stool
on PBS
drowned & buried

in a privatized
safe deposit box
of toxic shock sewerage
wearing a body bag
on his head
instead of a shower cap
him head big & blowed up
like a alligator float
in the Mardi Gras
stealing Christmas
from children
not yet born
cock blocking the breast milk
of Welfare mothers
replacing it with asbestos,
comparing hungry babies
to alligators & wolves
(if that's not the pothead
calling the kettle a crackhead!)
his ass adorned
with the manicured hands
of the rich rubbing him
for good luck
like a white Buddha
or fist fucking him
with their pinkie ring on
like the greasy
pink piggy bank
                he is
  grinning
through a grimace
with shit stains
on his teeth
& dollar signs
on his tongue
lapping
& lashing
out deform
after deform
after deform

You Can Bet Your Bottom Dollar

What is the surplus value
of your skull cracked in two
your ass split open on concrete
your lungs black as coal
skin tar & feathered
arms flapping about
like a butterfly with clipped wings
trying desperately to salute the flag
hands clasped together by nails
praying to a god who is not there
handing your life over
to those who do not care
whether you live
or die

What will the Dow Jones
Industrial Average ring up
when your child does not
come home from school
when you find out your doctor
is a fool and the nursing home
staff let your grandfather
drown in his drool when your
toilet water starts glowing in the dark
from your radio active stool

Zen

Are you waving the flag
or is the flag waving you?

≈

Coltrane Spoke To Me One Night

≈

Coltrane Spoke to Me One Night

What came out of his horn
was murderous, the world
come undone in the belly
of his song. Sound
cursing the night
for centuries of insomnia,
the mirror persecuting
the image, crucified
and lied to, tied
to railroad tracks
of bones at the bottom
of the sea, wrapped
around the earth
like moss on stone,
this is the breaking off
of locks and chains,
this is the skin toughening
up to break the needle.
This is what it means
to be alive, awake, sober,
feeling the welts and whip
marks evaporate from the flesh.
We are numb and feeling.
We know what death tastes like.
We will stay awhile
and be your worse nightmare
if that's what it takes
to sing our song.

I want to float through you

On a raft made of skin
Pass prayers through your lips
Toward the cathedral of your bones

On a Greyhound Bus from Detroit to Dayton, Moving Towards 33, After Reading a John Ashbery Book

You never quite catch it,
the thin hand of the clock
making its way round the
numbers, pushing the big
hand forward another
notch, the first gray
hair that springs
out of your mustache,
taunting you in the
mirror, your child
getting taller, your mother
older, time and space
and gravity collide,
unnoticed except
in the body, with
its creaks and stiffness,
the flesh soft and vulnerable,
the skin, just as soft. Time
sticks and moves
like a prizefighter
catching you off guard
as you wake from
dream or nightmare,
gasping for air, because
in your conscious or
unconscious mind, you
suddenly pay attention
to your own breathing,
and think, perhaps,
that you had forgotten
how, or that you
were never really
breathing at all.

LIGHT

It was there where the eyes
are first exposed to light
where you learned to adjust them
those first few waking hours
when you come out into the world
kicking and screaming,
only you did not kick,
or scream—just wondered
even at that pale age—
when almost nothing has been
etched upon the brain, but pain—
that you learn to adjust your eyes
to the light that quickly replaces
the space your mother occupied
when her eyes tried to avert yours
as the nurse lifted you to her chest,
wondering why the light was so sharp
and stabbing, the room emptier,
and if your mother
would ever come back
to claim you.

a Date with Poetry

35 came on me
like a migraine
at 3 in the morning

I sat in silence
with an unlit joint dang
ling from my bottom lip

afraid to smoke it
prematurely, waiting
for what—

I'll read some poetry,
sit quietly in my
brown chair in search

of prayer in search
of something else
to move me, keep me company

besides the lazy droning hum
of the fridge and computer.
This is my favorite time

to be self-conscious and
melancholy, to peel
back years and wonder,

*Damn, where did it all
        go?*

35 just slipped up on me
like a woman I wanted
to bed, but changed

my mind, opting to jack off
instead—intimacy
carries its own separate set

of consequences onto the boat.
But I want to float—to
mope—to wallow in my own

dry, creaking bones,
where did all the time go?

I wish I could stay awake
forever and read till my
eyes disappear. *35,*

are you still here?

When Your Kisses Touch My Peas

what to do when your kisses
touch my peas baby please
baby please touch my
nape touches you
between your knees
with your fingers
in my hair twisting
and twirling bees wax
everywhere
                    what to do
              when your
lips on my neck
like the sun and
my fingers trace the
space between your
toes for fun and my scalp
is loving you twirl
your fingers through
my hair devil-may-
care caress and coo
on this stoop in the shade
the leaves from the trees
make when I'm with you

Sometime in the Summer There's October
for Staci

though it's summer
i'm thinking of fall,
thinking of fall,
walking in the rain
on my way to you

I

i always liked the fall
walking down the street
in gray light afternoon
the leaves rising up off the curb
falling through the trees
a sunny somber Coltrane melody
rocking back and forth inside my skull

i always liked the way you smiled
sipping hot tea
in warm empty cafés,
windows clouded wet
with the memories
of your poetry

II

in the hospital room
your blinds are shut
so the light won't eat
into your bones

you lie in your bed
folded hairless
in a puddle
of dead skin

your sheets are soaked
in sweat
your pillow full of snot
and tears

and though they carve you up

into a jigsaw puzzle
of your former self
you refuse to sew yourself up
from the world

III

you smile at me
as i clown for you
as i clown for me
unable to swallow
this image

IV

what impostors we are:
you in that broken skin
trying to hold your bones
together in its web
of dust and blood

and me trying
to keep
from sobbing
like the night
my grandmother died
in her light blue robe

V

you try to talk,
your smock dangling
off your bones
as your laughter shifts
the light in the room,
the blinds masticating
the sun, and you
forcing out a smile
through the impostor
that traps your soul

in my eye's spying
examination

of what is now you
there is still
the you
i remember
with quick bright eyes
and attitude
the lips i've touched
the toes my tongue remembers,
that one sunny Sunday
in blue socks
that curled
as we baptized each other
in poetry,
the music
the wooden floor made
against your skin

how i wanted
to keep you
in *that* light

VI

but here, now,
you are in a dark cell
on death row,
a political prisoner
in Life's endless Kafkaesque nightmare
always absurd and unfair,
playing Russian roulette
with your sanity,
your sense of reality

Death, the final judge
and jury
Death, the governing body
with the power
to absolve
and release
and heal

and Cancer,
the prosecuting attorney,

trying to exhaust you
of your appeals
to live
leaving you with no other option
but to put yourself
in the hands
of bone marrow transplants
and corporate science
and other people's
blood

and though my days
are not as uncertain
as yours
if i could i would
will you them

Sleep

There is nothing more to say
when death leans its crooked face
on your shadow, nothing more,
nothing more to say
when time disrobes its skin
and you lay your dry flesh
in the cold flat cracked smile
of the earth like a damp towel
slumped on the bathroom tile

Nothing more to say
when your bones collapse
into dust like a steeple
of playing cards
and what is left
of you, your last few bits
of air unfurled and
whisked away
like a whisper
of a dream:
your conscious
emerging from the dark
luminous sea of sleep
to evaporate from you

When you are pushed out
of you, life's endless
unraveling, its constant
birthing,
there will be nothing
more to say.

When finality
no longer
exists,
nor you.

What was said was said:
impressions left behind
put down and recorded
into the memory

of your love's ear.

What was said
recedes from
what you thought
was you.

Death ties you down

                              to a hospital bed
with an IV tube, it presses its lips
against the flat of your stomach
tracing the tight skin wrapped
around your ribs. Death washes
its face in the puddle
your sweat makes.
You always fancied yourself
Blanche DuBois,
this time you get to be her,
relying on the kindness
of strangers, slapping
your arm for veins.
Death is tugging at your blood
like drawstrings. Blanche helped into
the white jacket by paramedics.
The nurse dances in to check your pulse
as Death sits on your chest,
collapsing your lungs.
What's it gonna be
this time, sailor?
The nurse says this to you,
winking her eye
while she slaps your arm,
watching the screen
flatline.

Black Orpheus

Death is disturbing the peace
Death is following everywhere
Death is in the air we breathe
Death is a fishnet reeling in light
Death is no more carnival
Death is a flurry of kisses to the brain
Death is a pit of boxes covered with dirt
Death could also be you drawing your blinds
Death is your mother laying on the floor
Death is the paint that never reaches the canvas
Death is the fanfare of worms and stars behind closed eyes
Death is silence disguised as black water
Death is your daughter collapsed like a broken doll
Death is a pair of lungs packed with mud
Death is the cobweb's echo rumbling in an empty belly
Death is Venitian blinds masticating the sun
Death is your broken cheek pressed against cold concrete
Death is the wailing open mouth scream of meat
    hanging from the butcher shop window
Death is the rat running in place, torn open on the bleeding glue trap
Death is grandpa unable to be awakened from his nap
Death is that rose that sleeps beneath your pillow
Death is the warm rain of schrapnel that drowns you in blood
Death is a low sky on one knee
Death is a tarpaulin of black slime coughing up black fish
Death is a tank that rests on a platform of bones
Death is the fragments of crushed skulls mistaken for bread
Death is a shirtless back pressed against the cold of the
    executioner's wall
Death is a canticle of moths climbing out of your open brain

Rio

when i was young
it didn't used to be
like this my brother

didn't always used to
smell like glue
mama never had

to worry about him
being caught
by the cops

for stealing
or finding his
body in the

street with
his head
cracked open

by a bullet

i'm twelve now
when i was young
i think i remember us
having food

& my hair
& my feet
being clean

& stroked
to sleep
by my mama's

hands

& not the fat white ones
of the tourist asleep
in the bed

who'll wake up
any minute &
pay me w/ his

drunken breath

& turn me out
into the cold
waiting for another john

when i was young
i hated the tourists
now i need them

& there's more
to choose from
though i have no choices

some of them
want to make it
with a pregnant girl

but i can't go on
like this i'll soon have to
find someone

to give me a heavy one
one with big shoes
& strong legs

one that'll make sure
that it'll only take
one kick

i can't afford
another baby

two years seems
so long

when i was young
life was less
complicated

american Hunger

there is beauty
in vacant eyes

wide eternal
dark spaces

where somewhere
somehow hope

lies

there is beauty
in abandoned

spots and
dirty spaces

where dreams
slip through

concrete cracks
and race along

hopscotch chalk
there has to be

some beauty
there where

solitary tears
crease the dirt

on a little brown
girl's face and

little boys
go hungry

playing cops &
robbers in

broken down lots
with nappy head

of hair and eyes
and eyes laugh out

despair

Mingus Among Us

Mingus Among Us

Mingus & his fatback bass
wide hips like wide eyes

strumming us & guiding us
stringing us & gliding us in

sweet sassy serenade
of pretty pirouetting ballerinas

a matador perhaps
standing Pithecanthropus

erect(us)

Mingus strumming
Mingus strumming

Mingus among us
Mingus among us

among us in Harlem
where we stand a

greater chance of living
in Bangladesh

among us in crackhouse
in trackmark dens

where dirty needles
gleam & wait in the sharp tooth

glare of deadly epidemics

among us with paramedics
scraping the stale vomit

of our dull suicides

corpses & zombies
arrested in bitter hate

bottled rage blues
frustrated arpeggios

muted Miles cantations
erratic muffled butterflies

stifled flutters
of the hip world

the bip bam be bop boom world
the cornucopia

of wet dreams &
elastic temptations

stretching skin for veins
tapping tapping

taptap tapping veins
like the drip drip dripping

of empty faucet illusions

Mingus among us
among us like Monk

Sphere T. Thelonious
Sir Duke of Funkdome

live w/ bebop bass
supremacy

slapping those ivory keys
like the bony necks of

Boston peckerwoods of ivy league
prep-school suck-ups & fuck-ups

gone frail in their numbered days
their desperate sun-rejected

melanin search for biological
supremacy in ill embarrassed

perversity
foolish toms gone

mad in their gray neck stretched
clean & taut   prepped

for the cutting block reality
of American dreams & nightmares

Mingus among us
among us like Trane

in burning prophet rage
of hypodermic duplicity

supremely loving us
struggling struggling

crucified by copyboys
for the guest oppressor

crucified by whiteboys
clumsy thieves who criticize

& teach & don't do &
can't do & can't mark time

& can't play a note
let alone pick up an instrument

fuck Bethoven &
fuck Bach &

fuck all those pale motherfuckers
shitted out of the bowels of Europe

rapists & imperialists culture thieves
& assassins, philosophizing & criticizing

bout Trane being insane

Trane was too quick for you un-hip
bankrupt ofays

too quick to conquer
rage like Bird bebop madness

Bigger Thomas pistol whipping
the heads of your Mary Dolton

white bitch Wonder Bread
Leave it to Beaver

okey doke bullshit aesthetic

Mingus among us
among us in alleys

& subways like flyboys
in buttermilk like strips

of yesterday's newspaper
blowing & collecting on

subway tracks & ammonia
pissed halls where we

kill each other off
for fake gold chains

& $100 sneakers
produced & manufactured

by the same motherfuckers
who sold your mother to the world

by the same motherfuckers
who cut the halfwhite baby

out your sister's womb

The Way We Move

the way we move, funk groove
beat the rhythm out some pavement,
our elegant violent attitude, quick
slow motion movement in quicksand
in somebody else's shithouse shanty town
shingly jingly chains clamped on our necks,
hang to the floor scrape spark and clink
and we make music out of this   cool behind dark
shades, taught to fear the sun, hiding in
beauty parlors and bars draggy face with
hatred and ugliness,
                            and it only comes when you don't
accept the natural gifts, the fingerprints of a
higher order of peace and simple logic, what makes us
phenomenal is that we can sleepwalk in
harmony, never breaking a sweat 'cept in factories
or bars, prisons we even build systems for, our
own street logic and survival, but this is not where
we're meant to be, not on the operating table of
extinction or at the broken doorstep of finality
stumbling drunk confused scagged out on whiteness
and greed and stupidity into the bleeding face of our
dead father, and we are not supposed to move
this way, slow mumbling suicide in quicksand and defeat
we must refocus, we must see again

In My Terrible Sadness

hunger blurs the eyes
where I read too much
the faces of my people
as they hump and strain
beneath the deceitful petty
tarpaulin of capitalism
that keeps us homeless
and hoping, that keeps
us penniless and shopping
for dreams to drink or
spill down the drain
the tears of our children
who play & scream hotheaded
frustration on stoops
in back alleys & crowded streets
where the stores are as full w/ merchandise
as the streets are of unemployed.

We can speak so many languages
and not understand despair,
fuck & shit without a care
and never understand our rage.

Please God, kill the Phone Company
Burn the factories, throw the TVs
out the window, strangle landlords
& insurance salesmen
and doctors who demand their bills
to be paid on time,
stab gov't officials in alleys
& limousines, destroy the
manufacturers of ultra sheen
& other cosmetic schemes that wish to sell us
pretty slick souped up dreams
when we in the middle
of some ugly wicked
shit.   Please God
     Please

No more time
for squatting
& biting our
asses in the
sand No more
hiding behind
metaphors
No more sitting for hours
and days in a filthy Welfare office
to wait to talk to people behind a desk
who just got off Welfare
and now have an attitude because you need
and they get paid to help you
and now want to deny you basic human needs
and put you through all types of brutal
unnecessary bureaucratic shit
for what?   so your kids can go
to sleep with food in their stomachs,
so they can have clean clothes
and books to read in a well-lit
house that they can call a
home and not a matchbox or closet
or rat-infested firetrap
to be burnt alive by corrupt insurance collecting
slumlords or get shot through
windows or paper walls by drug dealers
or runners who are nothing but low paid
lackeys pushing dead dreams for the
mafia & the gov't (which is redundant)
to keep poor people poor & sedated
& non-procreated & hated & hated
for the color of their skin or the
language that they speak & the food
& the music & the rhythm that they dig,
which is life which is life.

Eyeless in Harlem

flowers maybe
where bloods be
where blood be
where bloods be
throwin down
where shit be
where shit be goin
down   flowers
     may
           be
where knees crack
on concrete piss
and stairs, stares
stare, staring out
at the vicious displaced
lie of time standing still, the old
lady with the swolled up
legs and wig dragging groceries
across a crowded pavement,
we spill out spill out into the street
mashing our faces into the dog shit
and jive of lives spent on stoops,
stooped in shadows of our own fear
and self-hatred, duped and chained
to broken dirty mirrors we spit
into.   what is the sound of us
the look of us the thought of us
that would allow ourselves
to be tricked
over and over
again
what is the gentle whisk of life
whistling through the concentration
camp of our eyes, all hope meshed
and mangled in the barbed wire fence
of possibility that would allow us
the simple luxury of the butterfly
metamorphosed from the ugly hairy
worm, struggling to be free.

136

Rhudine Rhudine

who did not love you
back in the days
when you used to be
laid out on street corners
and in alleyways
in your half-drunk
blackout blues
who kicked you out
when you were only
thirteen
and who filled you
full of heroin and
sperm, sent you hurling
in your nappy head
despair calling you
ugly, kicking you
in your gut, spitting
your face
rhudine
i saw you shuffling
in your half-trod
down beaten walk
cradling a bottle
of beer beneath
a bloated arm
i saw you shuffling
in your plaid shirt
and burgundy cuffs
scraping beneath
your swollen shoes,
you turned to smile
and your huge brown
pupils drowned
in a yellow sea
of pain, rhudine
or was that the
blues singing in
your eyes or was

that the blues
singing in your
eyes or was that
the blues singing

Downsize Days

what do you do
when the dough
just won't do
when your check
just won't cut it
and your boss
wants to cut you

what do you do
when all you want
is a raise beyond
the 9-to-5 blood
pressure daze
where life is a tailspin
never-ending monotony
of sink and spend

what do you do
when the dough
just won't do
when your check
just won't cut it
and your boss
wants to cut you

what do you do
when all you want
is a raise
but all you get
are downsize days
where your check
is lowered
into the ground

what do you do
when your employer
becomes your mortician
and sends you home
with flowers
in a car
with no ignition

in a box
in the ground
to seal all traces
of recognition
that you may have employed
before that fateful day
when he turned to you

as a hangman dangling
a noose—as the mortician
opening the mouth of the coffin
to say: *Try this on for size.*

THE SECOND COMING

It was the second coming
of the sun
when once again
we were one
with the air
and not opposed
to breathing
when we were no longer
afraid of sunlight
and did not leave
our bones and skin
in the sand
when oil drums
were not buried at sea
and fish did not find
themselves belly up
on slime and debris
when the sidewalks
were no longer lined
with human flesh
and birds did not
bang their beaks
on the plastic face
of the wind or die
of black lung disease
when children
no longer rode
the pant legs and
cuffs of tourists
for money
to fill their bellies
with fumes of
airplane glue
It was when life
no longer had
an expiration date
and we were no longer
crash test dummies
with bar-coded tongues

and Alupent inhalers for lungs
when our hopes and dreams
and memories were no longer
faxed or e-mailed through
cyberspace schemes
and we found a better
means to communicate
and co-exist
with the possibilities
of human compassion
It was when cows
no longer keeled over
at the bump of a fly
and flies were no longer
offended by radioactive dung
and we did not depend
on rats and roaches
to pick up cable TV
It was when electricity
was no longer a dirty word
or a dozens joke to say
your mama's dead
It was when violence
was no longer a spectator sport
and kindness something you got
if you won the lottery

OUT OF THIS WORLD

I can dig those days
when we were not afraid
of the sun
where water rode
elevators of air
blowing cigar smoke
mushroom clouds
into the clear blue ocean of sky
where fish did not float
belly up atop
a black tarpaulin
of slime
and you did not have to
carry an extra supply of
backup refill lungs
in your book bag backpack
or briefcase

I remember
when plant life
was not scarce
as dinosaur shit
some lame archeologist
mistook for bones
But where are we now
blood peeling through skin
skin shrinking back
split open
making room for bone
melting in the sun
What are we going to become
mashed down cigarette butts
and ashes, smoke rising
up out of our asses
emitted up into the
stratosphere
out of the ashtrays
we call home

Bits of Silence

It's hard to talk when parts of your body are spread out into different rooms of your house, hammered out into separate pieces by the village blacksmiths, your soul evicted from its meat encasing. You search for it in the 'fridge, but its not there. Nor is it in the glove compartment of your car where another is waiting, hiding in the back seat, veiled by the dark of the garage waiting to jab your flesh, what's left of your soul leaking out from beneath the crack of light the garage door makes, letting out trickles of carbon monoxide, just enough to keep him conscious, to force you under with each violent hump. But rape is sport in this country, like hunting deer or skinning rabbits, or shooting ducks from the sky. You have it down to a science. Every time you walk out the door. The catcalls are cum shots from across the hall of your favorite church where the priest fondles little boys in confessionals or makes young girls wet their drawers. How you end up on stage in a bar dancing for old men to covers of Frank Sinatra tunes, you never know. But the pay seems good for what it's worth. They pitch pennies into your mouth and crotch, your legs stretched along the shoulders of the bar (like the broken silhouette of a corpse) where old men nod off into your crotch, snoring memories of your dead father forcing you to play house. The anesthesia still on his breath. The blood of your menses that first day destroying the sheets your mother washed in the bathroom sink with bleach along with her silence, for many years broken, glued together by Valium and booze, watching you crack like a teacup in her hands from the silence. But now she can't even watch you from where she stands staring out a window waiting for the nurse to feed her or change her diaper. The village blacksmiths got her too, even at her age, leaving their dead sperm in her dry sack like ants or worms or cobwebs of dust, memories to take to the grave, bits of silence stockpiled beneath the earth pushing up the flesh and bone of slaves, crawling in and out of her frame.

Oui Oui C'est La Vie
for Marc Oriol

the barbed wire fence passes through my blood
evaporating my flesh split like confetti
I am watching this parade of violence
like a silent movie in slow motion
the whites of my eyes are pendulous
my thighs rubber as the world tumbles
about me buildings colliding into clouds
clouds spinning around like fat clumsy pigeons
a mad procession of guards with barbed wire smiles
this is the celebration of death
I've always longed for
someone is tying my hands behind
my back another is holding me down
another is sweeping my feet off the ground
the soldier pounding the stone on my back
must think I always wanted to die
like this

Harlem to Havana
for Che

what does it take
to pump some blood
through the veins
of a tree
to get the grass
to sing
to spread air
along a river
of dry lungs
what does it take
to share a piece
of bread
to wrap some meat
around some bones
to bend the wind
into violins whispering
goodnight kisses
into the ears
of sleeping children
what does it take
to plant some flowers
in the skulls
of fading corpses
to ensure that backs
do not become launching pads
or stepping stones
what does it take
to extend a hand
to wet desert lips
with tears instead
of sand
what does it take
to fill a baby's belly
with songs

Before Sunrise

small songs crowd the hour
as I am close to empty
close to shutting down
no one to grab me
from the clutches
of the trap

I lie awake
fighting sleep
dreaming of being curled up
in my mother's lap
small songs crowd the hour
as I am close to empty
wanting to end it all

Eve's Bayou

what we have
are memories

the sad lyric
of a little song

the scent of swift
perfume

thoughts to embalm
the heart

like a stopwatch
in the palm

what we have
only lasts

as long as
we do

bending here

in the hands
of grass

What We Leave Behind

you leave your face in other peoples'
minds, though you don't know which
picture they take with them, which angle
they remember, which memory of you
they hold onto,
the teeth slicing glance
of a smile, your little kid
laugh, the eyes
in haunting somber
brood, you don't know
which mood they play back
and freeze frame, you don't know
you don't know
which impression
you leave, which note
you belong to,
not even
when they say
I love you.

BLOODSONG

Didn't I tell you
that the heart
is a mouth
on paper
that the paper
is a flame
split into lips
pursed like an arrow
and that arrow
bleeds into the drum
of one's tongue
trapped in memory's ear
Didn't I tell you
it is hard
for the wound
to forget
the migrating blood
forced out
by exile
or eviction
that one man's journey
is another man's
fast removal
from the face
of the earth
that some travel
in the hulls
of slave ships
while others
hug the bottom
of rafts
swallowing
oceans
of mud